IOWA

Anita Yasuda

www.av2books.com

LET'S READ
AV²
BY WEIGL™
ADDED VALUE • AUDIO VISUAL

Go to **www.av2books.com**, and enter this book's unique code.

BOOK CODE

Z 6 9 6 0 3 6

AV² by Weigl brings you media enhanced books that support active learning.

AV² provides enriched content that supplements and complements this book. Weigl's AV² books strive to create inspired learning and engage young minds in a total learning experience.

Your AV² Media Enhanced books come alive with...

Audio
Listen to sections of the book read aloud.

Video
Watch informative video clips.

Embedded Weblinks
Gain additional information for research.

Try This!
Complete activities and hands-on experiments.

Key Words
Study vocabulary, and complete a matching word activity.

Quizzes
Test your knowledge.

Slide Show
View images and captions, and prepare a presentation.

... and much, much more!

IOWA

Contents

This is Iowa.
It is called the Hawkeye State.
The name "Hawkeye" may
come from Chief Black Hawk.

This is the shape of Iowa. Iowa is in the middle part of the United States.

Where is Iowa?

Canada

N

W E

S

Pacific Ocean

United States

Atlantic Ocean

Mexico

Iowa is bordered by six other states.

The wild rose is the Iowa state flower. It grows in meadows and woodlands. This flower makes a fruit called a rose hip.

The Iowa state seal has a soldier, an American flag, and a cabin.

An eagle sits at the top of the seal.

OUR LIBERTIES WE PRIZE AND OUR RIGHTS WE WILL MAINTAIN

IOWA

The state bird of Iowa
is the Eastern Goldfinch.
The Eastern Goldfinch
often stays in Iowa
through the winter.

Goldfinch eggs
are light blue.

This is the biggest city in Iowa. It is named Des Moines. It is the state capital.

The Iowa state capitol building has a dome made of gold.

Corn grows in Iowa. Iowa corn is sold all over the world. Corn takes five to six months to grow.

One ear of corn has about 600 kernels.

People visit Iowa to travel the Great River Road. The road is next to the Mississippi River. Forests, cliffs, and historic places are found along the road.

21

IOWA FACTS

These pages provide detailed information that expands on the interesting facts found in the book. These pages are intended to be used by adults as a learning support to help young readers round out their knowledge of each state in the *Explore the U.S.A.* series.

Pages 4–5

Iowa is an American Indian word meaning "the beautiful land." The state was named after the Iowa Indians. Iowa's nickname, the Hawkeye State, may honor Chief Black Hawk. He was leader of the Fox and the Sauk Indians in the early 1800s. Others believe the nickname came from a character in *The Last of the Mohicans*, a book by James Fenimore Cooper.

Pages 6–7

On December 28, 1846, Iowa became the 29th state to join the United States. Iowa is located in the center of the United States in an area called the Midwest. Iowa is bordered by Minnesota to the north, Wisconsin and Illinois to the east, Missouri to the south, and Nebraska and South Dakota to the west.

Pages 8–9

More than 20 American Indian tribes have lived in Iowa at different times. One of these groups was called the Iowa, or Ioway. This group gave its name to the state. The Iowa people lived by hunting animals such as bison and growing crops of corn, beans, and squash.

Pages 10–11

Wild roses grow throughout Iowa. On May 6, 1897, the wild rose was made the state flower of Iowa. Wild roses come in different shades of pink and have prickly stems. The state seal includes symbols important to Iowa in the background, including a plow, a rake, and a wheat sheaf. The Mississippi River is in the background, with a steamboat.

Pages 12–13

The Iowa flag was adopted in 1921. Mrs. Dixie Cornell Gebhardt, a member of the Daughters of the American Revolution, designed the flag. The flag's blue, white, and red stripes stand for loyalty, purity, and courage. The bald eagle holds the state motto, "Our liberties we prize, and our rights we will maintain."

Pages 14–15

The Eastern Goldfinch, also known as the American Goldfinch, is found in the fields and woodlands of Iowa. They often stay in the state through the winter. Goldfinches build cup-shaped nests. Insects and small seeds, such as sunflower seeds, make up the goldfinch's diet.

Pages 16–17

Des Moines became the capital of Iowa in 1857 because of its central location where the Des Moines and Raccoon rivers meet. The biggest employers in Des Moines are the state and local governments. The Iowa state capitol building is topped with a tall dome that is covered with 23-karat gold leaf.

Pages 18–19

Iowa's fertile soil, moist climate, and long growing season make it an ideal place to farm. Iowa has more than 92,000 farms. Ten percent of the United States food supply comes from Iowa, and a quarter of Iowa's farm products are shipped overseas. Crops such as wheat, oats, corn, and soybeans are grown in Iowa.

Pages 20–21

Tourists come to Iowa to enjoy the natural beauty of the state. Iowa is part of the Great River Road, which is a scenic byway that goes through 10 states along the Mississippi River. Beautiful scenery, museums, parks, and many historic sites, such as American Indian burial mounds, are found along the Great River Road.

KEY WORDS

Research has shown that as much as 65 percent of all written material published in English is made up of 300 words. These 300 words cannot be taught using pictures or learned by sounding them out. They must be recognized by sight. This book contains 55 common sight words to help young readers improve their reading fluency and comprehension. This book also teaches young readers several important content words, such as proper nouns. These words are paired with pictures to aid in learning and improve understanding.

Page	Sight Words First Appearance
4	come, from, is, it, may, name, state, the, this
7	by, in, of, other, part, where
8	American, and, earth, first, group, houses, Indians, live, made, one, people, to, was, were
11	a, an, at, grows, has, makes
12	also, on, white, with
15	are, light, often, through
16	city
19	about, all, over, takes, world
20	along, found, great, next, places, river

Page	Content Words First Appearance
4	Chief Black Hawk, Hawkeye, Iowa
7	middle, shape, United States
8	wood
11	cabin, eagle, flag, flower, fruit, meadows, rose hip seal, soldier, top, wild rose, woodlands
12	motto, ribbon
15	bird, Eastern Goldfinch, eggs, winter
16	building, capital, capitol, Des Moines, dome, gold
19	corn, ear, kernels, months
20	cliffs, forests, Mississippi River, road